THE ICE-PILOT SPEAKS

Also by Pauline Stainer

Little Egypt (Smith/Doorstop Books, 1987)
The Honeycomb (Bloodaxe Books, 1989)
Sighting the Slave Ship (Bloodaxe Books, 1992)

PAULINE STAINER

✦

THE ICE-PILOT
SPEAKS

BLOODAXE BOOKS

Copyright © Pauline Stainer 1994

ISBN: 1 85224 298 1

First published 1994 by
Bloodaxe Books Ltd,
P.O. Box 1SN,
Newcastle upon Tyne NE99 1SN.

Bloodaxe Books Ltd acknowledges
the financial assistance of Northern Arts.

Cover printing by J. Thomson Colour Printers Ltd, Glasgow.

Printed in Great Britain by
Cromwell Press Ltd, Broughton Gifford, Melksham, Wiltshire.

For Michael and Diana

Acknowledgements

Acknowledgements are due to the editors of the following publications in which some of these poems first appeared: *Aquarius, Bête Noire, Fine Tuning, The Frogmore Papers, Lancaster Festival Poems '91* and *'92, Manchester Poetry 4, The New Poetry* (Bloodaxe Books, 1993), *New Welsh Review, The North, Odyssey, Owl, Oxford Magazine, Poetry Book Society Anthology 2* (PBS/Hutchinson, 1991), *Poetry Review, Poetry with an Edge* (Bloodaxe Books, new edition, 1993), *The Rialto, Sixty Women Poets* (Bloodaxe Books, 1993), *Skoob Review, South West Poetry Anthology 1991, Spokes, Staple, Tabla* and *Verse.*

The sequences *Frequencies, Sanctuary* and *A Blind Man Passes La Sagrada Familia* have appeared as Carnivorous Arpeggio Press pamphlets. 'Kettledrummer' was included in *Up on the Roof / Little Egypt*, published by Smith/Doorstop Books in 1987. 'Sarcophagus' was commissioned by *Making Waves*. 'The Ice-Pilot Speaks' won first prize in the Skoob/*Index on Censorship* competition in 1992.

I would like to acknowledge the influence of Danah Zohar's *The Quantum Self* (Bloomsbury, 1990) on several of the poems in this book. Some poems draw upon other sources, in some cases a whole work, in some a particular line or sentence: 'The Ice-Pilot Speaks': George Mackay Brown, W.H. Auden, Franz Kafka; 'Frequencies': Edith Sitwell, V.S. Naipaul; 'The Bloodline': Stephen Hales; 'Christ in a Chimerical Landscape': Lancelot Andrewes; 'Snow on the Reclining Buddhas': Sir Thomas Browne; 'Iceman': W.B. Yeats; 'War Requiem': Bruce Chatwin; 'Bird in Space': Brancusi; 'Quanta': Barry Lopez; 'The Infinite Act': Lancelot Andrewes, Richard Crashaw.

Contents

The Ice-Pilot Speaks

I

No such thing
as a routine death –
in *ultima thule*
the shaman stretches
the throat of a walrus
over his drum.

It is Ascension week;
the men wear black crêpe veils
against snowblindness,
the ship's astronomer
is given four ounces
of raven;

sterna paradisaea
is caught with ordinary cotton;
a number of snowy owls
are shot,
one thawing its prey
against its breast.

O terra incognita –
the tundra is silk-crewel work;
polar-bears sweat
through upturned paws,
the ship's figurehead
warm as from the furnace

the sagas redden –
on tinted lantern slides
Amundsen drives
five of his dogs
to death
Language, open the sacred quarry.

II

I dream of your body
when there is no open water
and the Inuit women
soften foxskins
with their teeth.

It was like drawing
without looking
at the paper
as I ran my hand
between your breasts

but you remembered the nuns
at the silk farm
blanching the cocoons,
teasing out
the single thread

raw silk running

III

i

Like Quakers
the icebergs recline
their nudes

the light from their viscera
so blue, addicts can
no longer find the vein.

ii

Gymnopédies
Satie seeking
the antique whiteness

the estuary
swinging its mirrors
at right-angles

a looking-glass quadrille,
pistons counselling
perfection.

iii

Disquieting muses –
subtext
of the deep keels

the bisque-doll
on the seabed
mouthing the Titanic.

IV

Is it minimalist –
the music
for a northern light

fleece growing along
a sheep's spine, lava slowing
under high pressure hoses

the ship's surgeon cutting flesh
from between the ribs of the dead
to feed the living?

What is the sound
for such interstices –
the Piper Alpha wailing

fenders on the Silver-Pit
blistering at
the golden scenario

those two divers on the spiderdeck
underwater
at the time of explosion?

V

The high scree makes one dream –
ptarmigan hunters
use the snow as reflector
where they roost unseen,
the eight Inuit mummies,
one with Down's syndrome.

The blood-group of mummies
can be determined;
so what is this slippage
when you put them up darkly,
the white dead
already meditating flight

and the hunters are silenced
not by the muzzle-flash
from a gun
but by that sense
of encounter
with their own coffin?

VI

What is song
when the shroud
is left unlaced at the mouth
and the arctic tern
has a radio transmitter
lashed with fuse-wire
to its leg?

What are footings?
Reindeer kneel
to the cull;
in Eller Moss
was found the skeleton
of a stag
standing upon its feet

At the magician's house
I carve ivory noseplugs
in the shape of a bird
with inlaid eyes.
What is the spirit
at gaze

the deerness of deer?

VII

St Brendan's monks
sail through the eye
of the iceberg.

At first, they ran
with the shadow of the land
through light bluish fog

later, by moonlight,
the ship caulked
with tallow, shamans

clashing over the Pole
as if to earth
any dead in the rigging,

and at dawn,
floes gliding by,
chesspieces in lenten veils

the sea a silver-stained
histology slide,
the O of the iceberg

whistling like Chinese birds
with porcelain whistles
on their feet.

Even in prayer
they could never replay it –
the purity of that zero

Varèse, playing
the density of his flute's
own platinum

the intervening angel
bearing a consignment
of freshwater.

VIII

Pestilencia!

The living wear
the black death
like windroses,
red for the quarter,
green for the half-winds.

Who says plague
is monotonous?
Christ turns
on Yggdrasill
under the strobe lights

I am my beloved's
his desire is toward me
and the dead stiffen
under their many eiders.

IX

In the North West Passage
William Newton, ice-mate,
hallucinates:

under the mosquito net
Marguerite
braids her hair

We sleep apart
as if we were dead

but o the searching
tongue of the sea

each time the muslin
billows the bed

a leopard coughs
in the camphor tree.

X

Up she rises –
the sunken softwood ship
with her dissolving
cargo of sugar,
fainter than
the eight hooves
of Sleipnir
on the albumen print
of the glacier.

Pittura metafisica
the mistletoe shafting
Balder; Borges
feeling the pillar
in his hotel room
at Reykjavik,
the Euclid of childhood
flowing through him
like serum.

One waterfall is extraordinarily like another
but for lovers
who kneel at its lip
and drink from
an unspilled moon
the source is altered
utterly,
until the painter,
erasing their figures

draws five strings
down the canvas
and hears from behind
the golden mean
the rasp of the salt-lick
as on the evening
of the first day
a man's hair
comes out of the ice.

XI

Sfumato!

The blue whales are flensed
by steam winch;
local reds
boil from the heart.

The whalers could be
gods, butchering
Balder's horse against
the midnight sun.

Loki is bound
with his own entrails
but who will wear
this smoking scarlet?

XII

We are close-hauled;
the narwhals hang
belly to belly
in the water.

I run my finger
through your menstrual blood
and put it to my mouth —
O Sigurd, who understood

the speech of birds
and slit the mailshirt
grown into her flesh
as Sigrdrifa slept

not a drop runs over,
but there is no room for another
and outside
the warm ice rafting.

XIII

They had no faint object camera —
whether they saw pack-ice or fog-bank
or mirage, will never be known

the weather not quite reliable,
leprosy
that white list in the sky.

So what made our love-making
the palimpsest
for all successive acts

when in the sedge-meadow
the gods are discovered
at chess

and give over
on their marvellous boards
the game that must be lost?

The Lady and the Hare

They would have you believe
she slept on bedrock
where ash roots the stone

that what startled silence
was not a buzzard mewing
but the huntsman's horn unblown.

When the hounds
broke from their thicket
they froze at her calm

sensed in the cold apse
of her breast
both the dove and the bone.

Today we started no hare;
downstream of the waterfall
found only her shrine

and how sternly
the warm hare is folded
inside her fierce gown.

Pointing Lady in a Landscape
(after Leonardo)

How can we read her simply
as she ghosts past
so entirely *rubato*
that water would wear
her impression
like an oculist's seal?

Is it the physiology
of the smile,
printed on silk
so thin
the image can be seen
from both sides

or the sleight
of quantum movement,
the verve
of her barely being there,
*the fate of all those lost
probabilities*

when given half a chance
she would swallow
the pearl of the moon?

Kettledrummer

(after Paul Klee)

One evening
in the excitement of drawing
he had the feeling
he was striking a kettledrum

at first
it was light pencil
for the light drum-roll,
a symptom to be recognised in time;

then rising-tension –
the mettlesome tympanist
feet raised
to the daemon-beat

tightened drumskin,
the timbre of trance,
head thrown back
in the groundswell.

Lastly
the kid-covered mallets
hollowed, as if to house
his bone-marrow

the drum as pulse,
and with canny timing,
the black flourish
of the fermata.

Frequencies

I *Kettle's Yard*
(for Jacqueline du Pré who played there)

Then came the courtier Death
saw how she held the cello
in embrace like a lover,
and remission
the fleet accomplice,
the harmonic pitched with bravura;

beyond
a rippling-stitch of light
over fen water –
white willow
cut in white bud
stripped with the sap rising.

II *Frequencies*

The burning-glass
swings in the sun,
rings under vibrato;

in the dry valley
musicians gather to find the sound
to which the stones intone;

below foxholes
the great frieze floats
across the calcite crystal –

the ammonite,
coldest of grave-jewels,
clear quartz where its body was;

such intrinsic music —
the pliancy of the lens,
the implosion of the geode —

we do not know
whether their answering intensities
are wounds or wide roses.

III *Mirror-Canon*

There is some kind of exchange always
tapestries flow like plainsong
in the cleansing river

light plays on the still-life with dice;
a window embrasure is refracted
through the halo of the Christchild

passing-soft the note between harmonies
love as a bundle of myrrh between the breasts —
passing-soft the note between harmonies

through the halo of the Christchild
a window embrasure is refracted;
light plays on the still-life with dice

in the cleansing river
tapestries flow like plainsong
There is some kind of exchange always

IV *Prism in a White Room*

i

For you,
I would take out
the prism in a white room

the oblique kindling
from buried Pharaohs,
a crystal inserted to lighten the face

Turner's late white canvases
of nothing, and very like
horizon lost in absolute calm

the arctic hare's tibia
notched like a gnomen
into calendar of the moon

trace-element from metalpoint,
a thin silver stylus
for the end of time.

ii

Anguish not gravity
flaws the crystal –
morphine frozen in the syringe

at the sheer threshold
of avalanche –
white steppe-foxes

stunned by
blunt arrowheads of bone,
their pelts undamaged.

iii

Mystery is mute;
the cores of ancient snow
burn and atomise;

with heavy dust-like bloom
the quince hang golden
into the frost.

V *Aôroi*

The Greeks had a word for it:
those whose death is untimely;
before the concert
the young cello-player
wears gloves against the chill.

It is not music
that disarms,
but notation
of fern-staves
through the breast-cage.

The dead are contemporary;
their instruments
still strung with their hair,
their leaping chords
still dividing the pulse.

We must comb for amber;
keep time
in order to lose it;
ecstasy
our grave estrangement.

A Study for the Badminton Game
(after David Inshaw)

Presentiment even here –
in the surrealist height of the trees,
the suspended shuttlecock,
the windless landscape.

From the observatory
at the top of the tall house,
you can see the bright unease
of banners above the topiary;

the yew-alley
going down to the river;
the pared moon,
the clipped pyramid.

How silently they play,
the girls on the lawn;
a guest clutches her garden-party hat –
Ophelia floats by.

Why is it
we watch the distraught
from the sunlit roof
with such terrible detachment?

The sun seems different when it submerges a Roman wall in light

(after de Chirico)

We excavate nothing
but the ambivalence of sunlight —
funerary urns
of free-blown glass,
unguentaria
of alabaster

glass-eels
rustling in pulses
under the pontoon bridge
where the centurion
fished the drift
in the Roman shallows

light is lapidary —
cisterns flood
like moonstones;
at the camouflaged quay
dazzle-ships
ride the enigma

we fire sounding rockets;
nebulae sing
from their nesting mirrors,
the sun coughs
down the catacombs
and in the fatal arcade

the salamander
sheds its skin.

Sprung-timber

It was windless
when the boy climbed
to the warm attic

documents were stowed
under the rafters,
pink files
with laces of green silk.

He knew he should not have looked;
found his father's death certificate,
felt the joists
spring in the heat

never told them
he had discovered;
but when they said
he was like his father
good with his hands

the spring
of the strung body
re-opened his heart.

Between Stations

Between stations
not anywhere in particular
you put your neck on the line;
the train was delayed
above the water-meadows;
an ordinary suicide said the guard.

For a moment no one spoke.
Looking out,
I walked the weir-gate after snow;
saw the young swans
dip to the meltwater
below the roar of the foam.

And I have remembered
the marvellous interlacing
of their throats
against an unspilled reach
not anywhere in particular
but between stations.

Oracle
(after Redon)

The head of Orpheus floats by –
mouth and eyes closed,
a shock of hair
in charcoal
against a white triangle.

Is it a casual affinity –
the silver swivel
at the neckbone,
Coleridge watching the stars
swerve into triangles?

Perhaps silence
is only the body listening,
Eurydice aching
for the rift
where her breasts once were

the white triangle
a rogue element,
the wondrous head
still assembling,
singing the rune.

Sarcophagus

Today
in that cold yellow pause
before the rape fluoresces,
I saw the blue glow
of plutonium

men in masks and boiler-suits
on the roof
of the sarcophagus
running, running
with divining-rods in their hands

nimble as matadors,
the sun catching
the sellotape at their ankles,
the speech of birds
graphite against the sky

the oracular dove
nesting
in the reactor.

Xochiquetzal

The firefighters of Chernobyl
lie naked
on sloping beds
in sterile rooms,
without eyelashes
or salivary glands

o death
take them lightly
as the Colombian goddess
who makes love
to young warriors
on the battlefield

holding a butterfly
between her lips.

One Flesh

We waited for the eclipse
in that short period of still water
between tides,
the moon worked-bone
above the run of the sea.

For two hours
the coppery twilight of earth's full shadow
pulled on her own seas,
the blood crouched
in its grave circle.

She could have drowned in her sphere
through the refracted light,
the slow commingling
of one body shrouding another
coldly, without bliss.

How beautiful they are
the compensating orbits –
the umbra
sealing the naked wax
in the solar wind.

It was then love
we eclipsed the small hours,
not simply your body
shadowing mine
but you in me.

The Dice Players

The painter has arranged them
around four light sources
as if the spilling of dice
were logical

the lutenist playing
lilac negatives,
the moment selected
for its obliquity

and outside the frame,
objects in melancholy
relation; dusk;
velvet revolution

an outbreak of cholera
at the masked ball,
lovers exchanging tongues
like matchless birds.

Beardsley at Dieppe

His hectic dust
haunts the casino;
he would come when
the tables were deserted,
the gambling rooms empty,
looking for something frivolous
in the presence
of abstracts.

It still intoxicates —
absinthe greening the sun
in an offshore wind,
the hot sweet haemorrhage
as on the dolorous page
Isolde drains
the scarlet philtre
from her glass.

The Bloodline

Did you have exotic ancestors
they asked
taking a syringeful
of blood
in the haematology department

and I thought of the retreat from Moscow –
soldiers bleeding their horses
into saucepans,
scooping the hot blood
to the melt of their mouths.

How close they are –
the hydraulics of the heart,
those early experiments
syphoning
from a stallion's belly

Then I took away the glass Tube
and let the blood from the Artery
mount up in the open air

The Doctor

(after Goya)

It is not sepsis
we fear
as he warms his hands
over burning coals
in a great salver;
terror is also
an affliction.

When he threads
the curved needle
with braided silk
we shall never know
which of his huge hands
stifled a scream
in the physic garden.

Christ in a Chimerical Landscape

Do the resurrected remember
the lilt in the blood,
the donor heart
of the red practitioner
who reduces bodies
to perfection

the meld
of pheromones
as Christ and the Magdalen
intinct the bread
and the yellow lilies lie down
with the snow-white lion?

Do they hear
the mercuric music
thin as cat-ice
as the bones vibrate
along the sightlines
of the serpent's skull

the wild bees
hanging like mistletoe
from the transom
before swarming
into the hole
in Christ's side?

The fountain
sways its root
when from the extracted body
bruises migrate
like birds
and the gardener

made her all greene
on the suddaine.

Burying the Green Boy

Japanese physicists gather
to study the crop rings;
they measure humidity,
electro-magnetism,
hoping for the occasional double centre;

they try so hard
with their ball lightning
apparatus,
simulating circles
in a plasma chamber

but the Green Boy
reaped the static here once,
where the round barrows
hold their foetal dead
like *chakras*

and they will not catch
the circle as it forms –
stalks whistling
with the moist wind
of the Apocrypha –

any more than they will catch
the edge of that moment
when he steps
from the intense spin
of the barley

slips a metal sleeve
on the whetstone.

Lot's Wife

She still asks
questions about rain
in the wind
from the Dead Sea

the oryx drawn
to her salt-lick,
the myrrh tree
oxidising

her handprint
redder than
blood–orange
against the rock.

But above her
on the thermals –
what concentrates
the lens

into the hawk's eye,
as she turns
on her axis
of crystallisation

calcium surging
through her cells,
the dry–brush stroke
over her orifices

seamless
as moonrise?

Mary on the Grass Bench

(after Dürer, 1503)

He has cornered her
on copperplate
in the enclosed garden

everything inverted
for the graver,
even time on its sapling

and he, childless
master of proportion,
did he feel the arrow

fletched with the sun
as she parted her fingers
round the nipple

the milk flowing
with *ankhs*,
Isis suckling her son?

Onnagata

The stage is white as a soda plain,
the kabuki actors
sashed with cinnabar.

Autumn ties its bloodknot;
circular jades
swing through the upper snow.

Between dancer and instrumentalist
the onnagata plays
a young girl returning

in the spirit of a heron,
his face so thickly powdered,
nothing can mask

the way his mouth
searches her breast
beneath the processional silks.

Snow on the Reclining Buddhas

They wear a white clay slip,
pure as the sound
of the two-handed sword
through the air

drawing their deep gust
of the world
when a bird presses primaries
into their snow

and behind them
where the sky clears,
the greenish glow
of a satellite dispersing.

Thaw

Why should meltwater
press so
on a wound?

The bodies of Victorian climbers
are recovered
as the glaciers retreat

erratics
in the malachite green,
backlit by the sun.

It can still open an artery –
that glimpse
of their release –

uncorrupted, roped-together
as if death
were a minor master.

Iceman

He didn't flow with the glacier –
but o the reciprocal dazzle

the dreaming of the bones
under the pneumatic chisel

the tail-flights of his arrows
still primed in the ice

and above, through the Saharan dust,
the eagle with the sunlit eye.

Axe

(after Michelangelo)

They have put the pietà
behind glass
because a lunatic
lopped-off the Madonna's hands.

I replay each stroke
in slow motion
as if the five principal wounds
were not enough.

She looks too young
to be his mother,
but at the swish
of the axe

the punishing red
on the white relief
floats the word
Take. Eat.

and she takes him
like a lover
on her tongue
back into her body.

Magtelt's Song

The sixteen virgins
come down from the gallows
to the *music of chance*,
cinnamon and cassia
falling from their yellow hair,
the sizzle of snow
in the holes
where their hearts once were.

Ah sister flesh,
when their hearts came out
and clouded the steel,
the wound sang the knife
until under the ice
a crystalline stone
rang in the inner ear
of the fish.

Oxnead Hall, Norfolk

Byrd composed here –
the dead rise
through the underair
on their sugarlift etching;

in the still-room
rose petals are drying
for the wedding
of the daughter of the house;

windows open simultaneously –
polyphony,
the sudden alembics
distilling Corpus Christi

and the bridegroom
who will play her body
without looking
at the music.

The Plunge

John Cross, George Eliot's second husband,
leapt from the hotel window on their honeymoon.

Was he running scared –
imagining couples
in sexual positions
under the Venetian red ceiling
at the bordello?

Anything can enlarge the heart;
the gondolas carry quills of cassia
across the scalding lagoon;
in the palazzo
they throw spices on the fire.

So was it static
as she disrobed in the light
off the mirror
and her ageing flesh
cast its apothecary's powders

or did her body
have the strange shimmer
of a photograph
imperfectly fixed,
the lamps hissing

the Grand Canal holding for a moment
more light than anything else?

The Carnation House

(after Eric Ravilious)

If only they would swerve a moment
instead of just grazing
the glass –
their essential oils
en grisaille
above the cistern.

But I, who look always
for the blood-seam,
detect in their slight shift
from the vertical
that hushed propagation
which engenders the dream.

Blue Poles

(after Jackson Pollock)

He used glass syringes,
threw them down
when clogged,
trod the glass into the paint

walked on waxed paper
over six yards
of expensive Belgian linen
fitfully for half a year.

Finally, he put in
the blue verticals;
and do they affirm,
like furniture projecting
into infinity

or was it that he remembered
how after the storm
his wife had to remove
the glass from his feet,
the studio candle-lit

the drunken poles
of the power-lines down?

The Parachute Factory

(after Paule Vézelay)

She would watch the parachute-making:
white bolts of raw silk
for weighting the light;

her delicate cargo
to earth
the pure abstract,

the rippling relay
of pallors
against the zenith.

But how fugitive –
finding the diagonal
that electrifies –

hang-gliders
in the wind at sunrise
each on a coloured axis.

Paragliding over the Spice Routes

It's as if the blood billows
over the parachute-shadow
on the sea

azure sensation
of gossamer-harness
along the skin

white terns diving,
the moving ruffle of shoals
just under the surface

an indigo upsurge
as the wind freshens
to the smoking horizon

and beyond the curving wake
of the speedboat
tensile, shining

vessels drawing their cargoes
into the haze
more whitely than adamant.

Turner is Lashed to the Mast

I did not paint it to be understood
but to show how water
makes the wind visible,
how the sea strikes
like a steel gauntlet

I scent the blizzard
lashed like Odysseus,
the air laced with diamond,
salt-pearl at my wrist

indistinctness is my forte
a gauze backdrop,
a ship hulling
to the hiss
of the vortex

I would fix
such sirens,
before unseen currents
disperse their dissolve.

Woolpack
(for Ian Parks)

Such pressure –
the fleeces packed
into the fen
under the floating church

supple as soil
below a monastery
layered red
with regular bleedings.

Are these the earth's
imagined corners –
the great number of fleeces
squared in a cloth?

And that settling –
is it silt through
the woolpack
at the Agnus Dei

souls gathered like fleeces
as they are shorn –
or the sluice
of the Golden Fleece

still holding
while the candles hesitate,
its particles
of pagan gold?

This Atomising of Things

In the dustless
centre of the lake
artisans sieve powdered
gold into lacquer

differing meshes,
spangled ground,
not so much fusion
as the smoke from it

ashore – beasts
of soft red sandstone
smouldering
along the spirit road

and the after-touch
of a girl warming
a pouch of silkworm eggs
between her breasts.

Lepers at Dunwich

Distance is different here –
between dissolvings –
dust fine as pouncing rosin
under the fresco
where the angels have lost their sandals

do not look at the lepers
but the spaces between –
the phrasing of spray
against sandstone,
martins mining the undercliff

attrition is
iodine on the wind,
the hairline eroded,
no purchase for the compass-point
to swing its halo

immunity
to ravish the unlovely –
even without lips
they are brides
of Christ

and he holds them
indissoluble
in the salt undertow
as if after the first drowning
there were no other.

Kinga Chapel

At the salt mine,
freshwater collects
into underground lakes;
those who cross by ferry
to the fireworks
wear river-pearls
that vaporise
into half-light.

Some take mass
beside the brine-wells.
Such crystal pressure –
the perfect acoustic
of the vault,
the percussion
of the blue quintet
against the bedded salt.

Salt Christ – the tallow
drips into the lake –
men carve green blocks
with miracles in relief –
your penitential harvest
seven soldiers
drowning in freshwater
above the virgin salt.

Fantasia for Virginals

*hardly one... boat in three that had the goods of
a house in, but there was a pair of virginalls in it*
PEPYS

They take the same slipway
as from the plague,
within musket-shot
of the flames;
a woman's skull
in the river gravels,
a floating mirror
as the crosswind flips up
the virginal's lid

the keys are witchwood –
but what is perfect pitch
when in the great frost
the children of looking-glass makers
fit the shin bones of beasts
to their feet
and with iron-shod poles
strike ever and anon
against the ice

and centuries later
in the molten aisles
of the ironmasters
the updraught
groans through organ-pipes
as the Crystal Palace hawk
beats against
the glazing-bars
with its boiling breast?

War Requiem

During the Lachrymosa
we could hear people hammering
bits out of the Berlin wall
And that other sound
of low voices singing

the Polish actress Mila Weislitz
giving a recital
in Auschwitz
against the flicker
of the crematorium

the orchestra
disrobing in the shower room
after a performance
of the Verdi Requiem
at Teresienstadt

and Britten's soprano –
did she hear
the perfect pitch
of crystals
infusing the gas chambers

her own octaves liquid
as those fluted glass rods
which when turned
give the impression
of waterfalls?

Threshold

I

Everywhere
the luminous inconsequence
of little interiors

Gwen John waking
to the unseen colours
of flowers culled at night

St Francis
preaching to the birds,
the quantum leap

of the stigmata
eight minutes ago
in the sun

the swan entering Leda
like laser
through alabaster.

What precipitates bliss
when nothing
is arranged

not even the sabre
in the frozen air?

II

He was flayed alive
after sacrilege –
his skin still under
one of the church hinges

the bees build
in his bone lesions
between the keyhole
and the later masonry

I detect
as by ultra-violet
their wax tabernacles
his viscera

that earlier torture –
the ribs broken
until his lungs winged
each side of the spine

even now at night
they give off
phosphorescence,
small fragrance

and beyond,
electrified vortices
of red and white
over the crop rings.

Sanctuary

I *Sanctuary*

We filmed by quartz lamp
where the hunters
kindled their limestone lamps
with lichen,
let their burning ochres drop.

The dappled horses overlap,
gallop with manes blown back
along the clay ledge,
the stag haloed
by a roaring cloud of his red breath.

We pan with the lens;
above scaffolding holes
the elect species
flow past
in their summer pelts,

musk-ox and unicorn,
aurochs on a calcite field,
the yellow foal:
a sponge of foetal skin
once hazed the mane.

We think we record everything –
pouches of pigment,
brushes of badger and fox,
a fluted bird-bone
for a flask;

but in that moment
when the heat from our cameras
still hangs on the cave air,
we hear it –
the percussion between ice-ages –

initiates
taking up their ritual instruments
under the frieze –
the struck shoulder-blades
of the mammoths.

II *The Mark*

We have dipped our boots in disinfectant;
under the resinous flare
of the pine-torches
the cave-lions extend their claws.

How narrow the crossing –
the lioness rolling a nugget
of golden ochre under her paw,
the absence of pollen on our feet;

our surgical notation
of blazon and grid,
the paired signs, male and female,
spear and wound;

the sound
of the trajectory of weapons –
the engraved stag
paralysed by flint-point,

tongue protruding
from the muzzle,
breath stippled
into earshot.

The great cats mount each other,
spit blood,
mark their territory
with jets of urine –

but what spurt is this
reddening the rock,
when the hand-axe
corrects the speared breast?

III *Sounding the Shaft*

The signs speak under the precision lens.
We meter the light, crop the print;
how the bone-marrow burns;

the lamps redden under the scaffold;
our picnic bones drop between the trestles;
the signs speak under the precision lens.

Here the hand was used as a template,
the air pungent with calf-tallow, green-juniper wick;
how the bone-marrow burns.

We reach by rope
the woolly rhinoceros who browsed on willow;
the signs speak under the precision lens;

the black bison
spills its entrails into the deep fault –
how the bone-marrow burns.

The man in a bird-mask falls back
from the heated oxides on the sacred ground –
the signs speak under the precision lens,
how the bone marrow burns.

Deer in Tuscany

Not just
a quincunx of aspens
lozenged
against the light,
but deer
running lightly between

and the desire
to staunch them a moment
between palings
as if they bled
with the strange formality
of a *Christo flagellato*

yet why make
an axis for wounds
when autumn is
so oblique a season,
nothing falls between
flight and its shadow?

The Intimation

I stood
with the headless beasts
on the parapet
of the palazzo

a far plough
creaking across the valley,
olives silvering
before the storm

the sparking tongue
of the bell above
disembodied
in the dumb mist.

Every angel is terrible
said Rilke
as the sheep glided
into one body.

I put my hand
on the stumps
of the blurred
leopards –

felt their sluice
of blood and rainwater
down the courtyard grille –
and behind

the hidden stairway
to the oratory,
Christ treading
upon the beasts.

A Blind Man Passes La Sagrada Familia

I

I have no spittle on my lids

I hear the light quadrupeds
squirrel, ferret
on the seven lesser altars

the sough of birds
chloroformed
with outstretched wings

still-born infants
rising on plaster dust
in the Santa Cruz hospital

the triple torchères
tossing their howling manes
for the three holy children.

II

I feel the flexible wire-mesh
of the recording angel
on the Field of the Harp

skeletons
practising deposition
from pulleys and weights

doves of polished iron
in the spandrel
as if heaven were to one side

the billow of incense
through the twelve bell-towers
each blowing a different death.

III

I sense the cranes rust
along their rat-lines, men like trees
walking the spiderdeck

the hare kindle
at the annunciation
in the bloody meadow

Lazarus
densify the ice-house
under the lawn

the desire to crucify
by mirrors, calvary flowing
until it floats

the pestles of the mortars.

IV

I see the masons
chip the stone
into blazing accidentals

the spires cast
their Venetian glass like falcons
into the wind

the seraph
at the empty sepulchre
in a suit of lights.

Bird in Space

It is not a bird,
it is the meaning of flight
the pale curve
to the underwing
earthed by the rainbow

the swivel and leash
of Egyptian falcons
slipped from a mummy's fist,
their night pricked
as for transfer

the flare
of honeywax birds
set alight
by the mass-candles
at which they sipped

the perfect pitch
of harriers
through stained-glass
browsing
from calvary

the quantum physics
of swifts
as they descend
footless
into the pentagonal garden.

Quanta

I

Reality happens
when you look at it –
the deer fawn
in the vertical light,
the crystal hunter
is killed by a single falling stone
on Annapurna.

But what perfects the casual –
Vermeer buried with three children
of unspecified sex,
the shaman in the glacier,
a crystalline disc pressed
to the strange blue tattoos
still intact on his breast?

II

Things happen
simultaneously
and in every direction
at once

hail drives
through the samphire
where the ammonites
show signs of healing

high-level
radioactive waste
is turned into molten glass
sealed in stainless steel

a pyx of white silver
is laid in a silken
compartment
in Christ's body

the limbs of mummies
crackle like chemical
glass-tubing
and give out great heat

the ovens work continuously;
no part of the prisoner is wasted;
dental gold is returned
to the Reichsbank

the city swings like a cradle –
the seven vials
spill their seven plagues
into the rubble

up above somewhere a fox crosses over
and the daughter of Jairus
is raised behind the geranium
on the windowsill.

III

What is for real
is the marvellous sufficiency
of the moment –
the automatic weapon on multiple lock –
electric plasmas
intransigent as angels.

Nothing is out of true:
purists whistle up
the bloodhounds,
those about to be executed
wear red blindfolds;

unhurried as lilies,
the disciples sit
at the holy supper
while the lovely boy
is hung *at a bough;*

no masking agent
for the heart
except insouciance –
the *mood indigo*
at the stroke of the green axe

willows breaking into F$^{\#}$ minor
for the flagellation
in a landscape,
the angel
at the inter-tidal funeral
announcing the end of time.

The Infinite Act

(after Stanley Spencer)

They are laying main drainage
in Cookham High Street;
the Queen's Swan-upper
nailed to the cross,
villagers craning
from the windows
like gazehounds at a tryst.

O the savour of Paradise –
as Adam names the animals
the leopards drop like honey
at their sweet difference;
stretcher-mules struggle
to rise for the resurrection
of the soldiers.

In the field hospital
dressings blush
into angelic orders,
forceps irradiate
the wound
the centre from which
all lines are drawen

What is charisma?
Love shirrs the petticoat,
the bride leans over
a chest of drawers,
Christ opens
the purple wardrobe
of his side.

But in the middle distance
Hilda has her foot
on the stile;
her husband's unanswered letters
stream past
terrible as a cloud
of witnesses;

the artist and his second wife
cannot perfect the error;
the disciples shoal
along the malthouse wall,
principalities and powers
smoke their bayonets,
Lord is it I, is it I?

Ave verum corpus
how do lovers know
one ecstasy from another
when they amaze
the moment
body to body
on the naked ground?

Thomas Traherne in the Orient

They shall look on Him whom they have pierced
clothed with the Southern Cross,
sun and moon on threaded rings
hurrying, tarrying

they shall hear
the blue cough of leopards
on feast days
in the bridegroom's chamber

they shall tongue
such syllables
the unicorn will kneel
to the Buddha

they shall see
young men
flex like angels
in the gem-mines

they shall sense
the seraphim
as elastic particles
rippling under haze

they shall dilate
like donors
before the sea-wind
in the cinnamon tree

they will be
such felicitous dust
in the balance
they will unsuppose

the body.

Gem-Dice from a Cinnamon Coast

I

The jetty is sprung
with split saplings,
the gourds warm-yellow,
the palm-tapper girdled
to the trunk.

Against the causeway
of crushed shell,
someone splits a coconut,
lets the milk
spill into the sand.

I no longer bleed each month;
but under the high salt tide
the barracuda run,
and downriver
village women prise open the oyster.

II

Natural to lie naked

Each act is different, you said,
the radiance of the body
barely begun

but I, glimpsing from the pillow
the moon lift
over the sill

the silted estuary beyond
where masted vessels
once thronged the river

knew the infinite act
to hold you in me
as I held you then.

III

We studied the night sky,
the gemmed axles,
the contained fires.
Easy, you said
to see Jupiter's second moon.

You gave me the glasses –
but how could I hold them steady
knowing at dawn
you would draw me out
like flame?

IV

It is over;
we drowse
as if purified;
the physicality
of miracle
to lie inward and naked;

but to contain
the urgency of innocence –
is there no lasting seal
when after ignition
hushed bodies
still burn?

V

How succinct the lovers –
they are pressed together like sweet kernels;
the warning bird calls all day long

under the hibiscus
they lie in their light trance
soundless as lizards

their kisses flicker,
mosque-swallows
blue-listing into the dusk

her breasts spice-islands
brushed
with vermilion.

If time is kept
it is by silken fuse
and trails of incense

the bee-eater
with liquid-yellow throat
strikes to remove the sting.

How succinct the lovers –
they draw from each other
that sweet extract which darkens with the season;
the warning bird calls all day long.

VI

The dark musicians
came over the night-sea
salt on the prow

they pressed their wild sweet stops
against the driving-silver
of the tide

the fire-eater
with throat thrown back,
smoke issuing above the surf;

such glancing accuracy
of flame along the flesh
I put my mouth to yours

and improvised.

VII

All day we waited
for the osprey
to stoop from the cross-mast,
clasp a burnished fish
in the flailing light

so how
between cinnamon coasts
could we have missed
that plunge
pounced with blood

a membrane over the eye
at the impact of entry?

VIII

Outside
with unseen accuracy
bats touch the skin of the water

inside – the smell of warm wax –
the urgent impress
of your body on mine

we are knit and reknit
like slow flares
in daylight

the moment timed
till it gives back
no altered echo

and upriver – the performing magic –
fire-throwers
exhaling the flame.

IX

The stilt-dancers
are blood-red
in the black night;
Orion overhead,
the young stars
burning hot and blue
the sand arena
blazing with cressets
and swirling, pleated silks;
the shaman
sliding gem-dice
under the lids

and beyond,
where the moon glitters
off the salt shrouds,
the lean, painted boats
swing from their moorings
on an inconstant tide.